NETWORK GREATER MANCHESTER

NETWORK
GREATER
MANCHESTER

MARTYN HILBERT

FONTHILL

Fonthill Media Language Policy

Fonthill Media publishes in the international English language market. One language edition is published worldwide. As there are minor differences in spelling and presentation, especially with regard to American Engl and British English, a policy is necessary to define which form of English to use. The Fonthill Policy is to use t form of English native to the author. Martyn Hilbert was born and educated in Great Britain; therefore, Britis English has been adopted in this publication.

Fonthill Media Limited
Fonthill Media LLC
www.fonthillmedia.com
office@fonthillmedia.com

First published in the United Kingdom and the United States of America 2019

British Library Cataloguing in Publication Data:
A catalogue record for this book is available from the British Library

Copyright © Martyn Hilbert 2019

ISBN 978-1-78155-767-9

The right of Martyn Hilbert to be identified as the author of this work has been asserted by him in accordan with the Copyright, Designs and Patents Act 1988.

Typeset in 10pt on 13pt Sabon
Printed and bound in England

Contents

Introduction   7

1   North and North-West   13

2   East and North-East   31

3   City Environs   47

4   West and South-West   63

5   South and South-East   71

6   Metrolink: An Overview   81

Bibliography   96

Introduction

Welcome to Greater Manchester. The large conurbation was a product of the Local Government Act of 1972, with the Metropolitan County coming into existence in 1974. Covering 492 square miles, the area has borders with the counties of Lancashire, West Yorkshire, Cheshire, Derbyshire, and Merseyside. It is home to 2.9 million people. Greater Manchester has a historic heavy rail system that has a 142-mile network serving ninety-one stations. The network not only includes the western end of the world's first true 'intercity' railway that opened for business in 1830 but also included the newest section of operational main line railway to open in the UK, when the Ordsall Chord was completed at the end of 2017. The area is also home to the UK's largest light rail and tram network, the Manchester Metrolink, the first part of which opened in 1992; it now totals 57 miles, having 124 stops on its busy and well-patronised system.

Within its boundaries, the Greater Manchester area has the highest total of motorway network than any other UK county, and both the heavy rail and light rail systems are an important alternative to the ever-congested road networks.

At the heart of the county is the ever-changing, prosperous, vibrant, and diverse city of Manchester. Recognised as the world's first industrial city, Manchester was once known as 'Cottonopolis' due to the high number of cotton mills, cotton finishers, warehousing, and the trading facilities for the buying and selling of cotton products and raw materials. At the dawn of the Industrial Revolution, the population of Manchester in 1801 was 88,000, subsequently soaring to 766,000 by 1931. The area also incorporated many of the well-known Lancashire mill towns—Bolton, Bury, Oldham, Rochdale, and Wigan—all of which played a major role in the success of the Lancashire cotton industry that was world famous and once provided employment for tens of thousands, with the railway network playing its role in making the area an industrial powerhouse.

Although over 30 miles inland from the coast, Manchester was connected to the Mersey Estuary and the Irish Sea by the Manchester Ship Canal. Opening in 1894, the huge feat of civil engineering enabled large ocean-going freight ships to reach the prosperous and expanding city via its large dock complex. The world's first industrial estate, Trafford Park, was located at the end of the Manchester Ship Canal, opening in 1897; the estate was served by 26 miles of railway system operated by the Manchester Ship Canal (MSC) Company. The estate was home to such names as Ford, Westinghouse, Metropolitan Vickers, Kellogg's, and the Co-operative Wholesale Society, who constructed large flour mills there. During the Second World War, some 34,000 Rolls-Royce Merlin engines for

Where it all started: the original Liverpool and Manchester Railway buildings fronting on to Liverpool Road, Manchester. In use as a passenger station from 1830 until 1844, the station area, buildings, and warehouses became a goods facility until closure in 1975. It is now part of the Manchester Museum of Science and Industry (MOSI) complex that celebrates the city and its historical railway and industrial heritage.

RAF aircraft were also produced at Trafford Park, with the Ford factory being turned over to war production. Post-war, changing patterns of trade, economic recessions, road transport via the expanding motorway network, and the gradual rundown of the Manchester Docks complex would see the MSC railway system finally close in 1998.

The Greater Manchester Passenger Transport Executive (GMPTE) came into existence in 1974, and in common with other large UK cities, the PTE was responsible for the provision of public transport including both bus and rail services, trying where possible to make the two different forms of transport to have some coordination and to ensure that the population of Greater Manchester could have a reliable and user-friendly transport system. In 1977, the GMPTE was the largest transport body in the UK, outside of the Greater London area. The bus network across Greater Manchester had been organised into one body back in 1969 as a result of the Transport Act 1968, when the SELNEC (South East Cheshire North East Lancashire) PTE was formed, to coordinate public transport in the area. During the period 1969–1974, the bus operations of Manchester Corporation, Salford, Ashton, Bolton, Wigan, Leigh, Lancashire United, North Western, Ramsbottom, SMHD, and Rochdale, totalling over 2,500 vehicles, came into the SELNEC fold, with the buses eventually gaining the corporate GM orange and white and the later orange and brown livery. When the Greater Manchester area came into being in 1974, all bus and rail operations then came under the control of GMPTE. The rail network that served the county in early 1970s was then still operated by British Rail, with the PTE providing coordination and subsidy; the visible change on the rolling stock was that the PTE 'M' logo appeared on the sides of some multiple-unit coaches. The Greater Manchester corporate orange livery was only eventually applied to the Bury line Class 504 Electric Multiple Units and first fourteen of the Class 142 railbuses (142001–142014) that were new in 1985, while some ex-Strathclyde (Glasgow) Class 303 EMUs and Class 101 DMUs that were transferred south of the border to the Greater Manchester area kept their Strathclyde orange livery, it being a similar match to the GM shade. In the 1990s, a Regional Railways/Greater Manchester livery (two-tone grey with an orange bodyside stripe) was applied to some Class 142s, Class 150s, Class 305s and Class 323s.

In 1972, due to declining rail patronage and increasing traffic congestion, SELNEC had proposed to connect the various rail routes that focused on Manchester city centre. They had a vision to have a double-track underground tunnel system that would link Piccadilly station to Victoria station, connecting the rail networks to the north and south of the city. The 2.75-mile new line would have had five sub-surface city centre stations *en route*, at Victoria Low Level, Royal Exchange, Central, Whitworth Street, and Piccadilly Low Level. It was envisaged that the tunnels (and the inward and outward routes) would be electrified using the standard 25-Kv AC system. To serve the new operation, it was planned to order ninety-six three-car EMUs (PEP type units, designated Class 316), with the maintenance facility at Longsight depot. Christened the 'Picc–Vic', the initial estimate for the whole project was around £9.5 million, but in those inflationary times, costs eventually soared to £180+ million; with repeated refusals by central government to underwrite the ambitious scheme, the stillborn 'Picc–Vic' was finally abandoned in 1977. Some of the scheme would later come to fruition with the Metrolink light rail and tram system in the 1990s and with the completion of the Ordsall Chord project in December 2017.

Increasing road traffic and city centre car parking issues were among the catalysts for the creation of Metrolink, the first section of which between Bury and Manchester Victoria (converted from the former BR route) opened for business in April 1992. An extension from Victoria along the streets to Piccadilly station followed later the same year, with additional street running from Piccadilly Gardens to Deansgate-Castlefield and onwards along the former BR route to Altrincham also in 1992. The Eccles route followed in 1999, along with some heavy infrastructure where the new route threaded across the former Manchester Docks complex. The short 0.25-mile MediaCityUK branch was an add-on to the Eccles route and opened in 2010. Routes to Oldham, Rochdale, and South and East Manchester were completed between 2009 and 2013. Ashton-under-Lyne, East Didsbury, and the airport followed in 2014, with a second city centre crossing being completed in 2017. Work is in progress to take the Metrolink across Trafford Park, terminating at the large Trafford Centre retail and leisure complex adjacent to the M60 motorway. This spur off the existing Eccles line at Pomona is due to open in 2020. The well-patronised system (41.2 million journeys were made in 2017–18) is now on its second generation of trams, with the original thirty-two Italian-built AnsaldoBreda T68/T68A vehicles being phased out in 2010–2012 in favour of Bombardier Austrian-built M5000 Flexity Swift trams, 120 of which currently provide all services across the system, with another twenty-seven vehicles on order. The yellow and silver livery that the fleet carries is now a familiar part of the Greater

Manchester street scene, one even featuring in the opening title scenes of the ever popular and iconic Granada Television/ITV *Coronation Street* series that is set in the fictional Manchester area of Weatherfield. The system is owned by TfM but currently operated by RAPT Group.

Following the privatisation of British Rail in 1996, the main provider of local rail services across the Greater Manchester network was First North Western (First Group) from 1997–2004, then Northern Rail (Serco-Abellio) from 2004–2016, and is currently Northern (Arriva Rail North) 2016–2025. Other passenger train operators that currently serve the region are Arriva Trains Wales (TfW since October 2018), Cross Country, East Midlands Trains (EMR, August 2019), TransPennine Express, and Virgin Trains (First Group/Trenitalia UK, from December 2019). The remaining freight operations are handled by DB Cargo, Freightliner, and GBRf.

In 2009, the publication of the Government 'Local Democracy, Economic Development and Construction Act' enabled the creation of the Greater Manchester Combined Authority, under which Transport for Greater Manchester (TfGM) was formed; from 2011, the PTE ceased to exist, with all transport matters coming under the control of TfGM.

With the completion of the Windsor Link back in 1988 that enabled trains from the north to access Manchester Piccadilly; the Ordsall Chord in 2017 allowing services to run between Victoria and Piccadilly; electrification of the historic Liverpool and Manchester Railway in 2016; Preston to Manchester (via Bolton) electrification in late 2018; the opening of the north-west rail operating centre (ROC) at Ashburys in 2014; and with future plans for high-speed services to access Manchester off the HS2 from Birmingham as part of the Northern Powerhouse project and a high speed route across the Pennines linking the cities of the north, the railway system—rather like the cityscape of central Manchester—has changed dramatically in the last twenty or so years.

The network is also on the cusp of a major renewal of the rolling stock that serves the system. The Class 142 Pacer fleet is due for retirement in 2019, with new CAF-built Class 195 DMUs due to be delivered in 2019–20, along with a new fleet of EMUs; the CAF-built Class 331 fleet will see the familiar Class 323 units, which have worked in the Greater Manchester area since new, extending their sphere of operation across the north-west.

Over the last ten years or so, the skyline of central Manchester has changed beyond recognition. High-rise apartment buildings have been built, enabling city living and creating an area that is still open for business well into the night, with many bars, cafés, and restaurants in areas that were once in the business and commercial sectors of the city.

What follows is a journey from north to south across the heavy rail network and a general overview of the Metrolink in pictures with detailed captions, through the years with some scenes, rolling stock, and liveries that have now passed into history. While I have tried to give a balanced coverage of the whole of the Greater Manchester area (the boundaries being the GM ticketing area), with a system so large and diverse, it is difficult to cover every operation and location in ninety-six pages.

In the selection of pictures, I have tried to give a mix of motive power, but the inescapable fact is that the oft-ignored multiple unit in its various incarnations are what has kept the system running over the last sixty years or so. All images prior to 2011 have been scanned from Kodachrome colour transparencies, with digital images from 2011 to the present day. Hopefully, this may give some inspiration for you the reader to get out and explore the busy system and its varied locations. Transport for Greater

Manchester has some good value, all-system day ticketing on both the traditional rail and Metrolink networks, which aid exploration of the area; details are available at the TfGM website: www.tfgm.com.

The production of any publication is a team effort; my thanks go to Alan Sutton and the team at Fonthill Media for having the faith in me and allowing another selection of my work to appear in print. Many thanks to my wife, Gillian, and to all the good friends who have been a source of help and encouragement. Finally, a thought for all the staff who have kept the steel wheels turning across the Greater Manchester network across the years and continue to provide services in an area that gives the population an alternative to using the car in these ever-important times when environmental issues are to the fore.

Martyn Hilbert
Lostock Hall, Lancashire,
November 2018

1

North and North-West

The small town of Blackrod, located on the route from Preston to Bolton, is on the north-western fringe of the Greater Manchester network. Blackrod once had a pair of connecting junctions to the nearby railway town of Horwich, now sadly removed. On 21 July 1982, Class 47 47472 was calling at the unstaffed station with the 12.20 Blackpool North to Manchester Victoria service, one of many loco-hauled services at the time, increasing capacity along this busy route, but also covering for the increasingly worn out and ailing first-generation diesel multiple unit fleet.

As is common with many locations along the Preston–Manchester route, what were once small towns and villages have expanded dramatically since the 1970s and are now dormitory areas for Manchester's workers. Subsequently, many stations have been upgraded and additional car parking facilities added. The small station at Blackrod was upgraded and modernised in 2012, although it has remained unstaffed. With the former stone-built goods shed as a backdrop, a pair of Northern Class 142 Pacers—142040 and 142035—were arriving with the 13.23 Manchester Victoria to Preston service on 26 January 2018.

Running at speed, Virgin Trains Class 47 47817 *The Institution of Mechanical Engineers* was running between Blackrod and Horwich Parkway with the 12.22 Preston to Penzance Cross Country service on a snowy 30 December 2001. The railway is paralleled along here by the old A6 trunk road and the M61 motorway.

The station at Horwich Parkway was opened in July 1999 and is located near to Junction 6 of the M61 motorway and is close to the large Middlebrook retail park and the Bolton Wanderers football stadium. The small staffed station has a 151-space car park. It is the only station in the Greater Manchester area that is owned by Transport for Greater Manchester (TfGM) and is leased to Northern Rail. Due to engineering work on the WCML between Crewe and Preston, a pair of Virgin Voyagers—221142 and 221114—were passing Horwich Parkway with the diverted 13.20 Birmingham New Street to Preston service on 14 July 2013.

Complete with a shunting pole across the buffers, Class 08 diesel shunter 08340 was stabled between duties at Horwich Works on 16 August 1980; at the time, the works required the use of four of these locomotives. The loco was surrounded by refurbished wheelsets and axles adjacent to the wheel shop, with what was once the main locomotive erecting shop visible on the left. The Lancashire and Yorkshire (L&Y) Railway opened the works at Horwich in 1886, and it was the centre of their universe. Horwich would eventually produce over 1,800 new locomotives for the L&Y, LMS, and British Railways, with steam locomotive production ending in 1957 with the completion of BR Standard 2-6-0 76099. The last steam loco overhauled at the works was Stanier 8F 48756 in July 1964. The last batch of Class 08 diesel shunters was also produced at Horwich, with the last example (D4157) emerging new in December 1962. The works also overhauled the Merseyrail Class 502 and 503, Manchester–Bury Class 504 and the Manchester–Glossop–Hadfield Class 506 Electric Multiple Units. During the 1960s and 1970s, the works became an overhaul facility for the then large BR wagon fleet. A new mechanised foundry was opened in 1978, but overcapacity within the BREL empire, saw the workshops close in 1983 although the foundry continued on. The remnant of the works was sold by BREL in 1988 and the rail connection to the Preston to Bolton line was removed in 1989.

In the late 1970s and early 1980s, Horwich Works completed many conversions of redundant BR Mk I coaches into departmental service vehicles and overhead line inspection coaches. On 16 August 1980, former Brake Second Corridor Coach (BSK) M34467, which was originally built by the Gloucester Carriage and Wagon Company in 1954, was in the process of being stripped for conversion into an overhead line inspection coach for the then ongoing Bedford to St Pancras electrification scheme. It would eventually emerge from Horwich numbered ADB975682.

A pair of Siemens-built Class 185s—185118 and 185109—were passing over Lostock Junction with the 10.00 Edinburgh to Manchester Airport First TransPennine Express service on 10 November 2013. The pair of tracks leading in from the extreme right are from Wigan Wallgate via Crow Nest Junction and Westhoughton.

Running along what was once a four-track section of railway, from Lostock Junction to Bolton, a legacy from the days when this route carried large amounts of freight, TransPennine Express Class 185 185121 was running between newly erected electrification masts at Ladybridge with the 10.56 Windermere to Manchester Airport service on 26 January 2018.

Northern Class 156, 156424 was stood at Westhoughton with the 14.56 Salford Central to Wigan Wallgate service on 30 March 2018. The small station is located on the 4-mile route from Crow Nest Junction (East of Hindley) to Lostock Junction (North of Bolton), and it is one of two former Lancashire and Yorkshire Railway alternate routes that services from Wigan Wallgate can access Manchester. The station gardens at Westhoughton have been developed and are well maintained by the 'Friends of Westhoughton Station' group that was formed in 2012.

On the former L&Y route from Wigan Wallgate, Crow Nest Junction is located just to the east of Hindley; it is where the two routes to Manchester separate and converge. DB Cargo Class 66 66152 was passing over the junction with the 07.25 Wilton to Knowsley empty binliner service on 14 August 2018. The freight has traversed the 13-mile route from Salford Crescent via Swinton that was opened by the L&Y in 1888. The pair of tracks to the left lead towards Lostock Junction via Westhoughton, a route that was opened by the Liverpool and Bury Railway in 1848. There was another route that once diverged here, running in a north-easterly direction (closed in 1965) towards Blackrod on the Bolton to Preston line. Such was the volume of freight traffic here in the past that the two Manchester-bound routes were once both four tracks.

A pair of Class 150/1 Sprinters—150144 and 150136—were stood at platform 1 at Hindley with the 13.23 Kirkby to Manchester Victoria service on 28 May 2016. The pair of units would travel via Westhoughton, Lostock Junction, and Bolton. Hindley station once had four platforms, reflecting the volume of traffic that passed through here. Platform 2 was once an island platform, and the other westbound platform edging can be seen on the extreme right of this view. The gardens at Hindley (including a miniature Windmill) are maintained by the 'Friends of Hindley Station' group.

Resplendent in its new Northern livery, Class 156 156420 was stood at Daisy Hill while working the 12.44 Kirkby to Salford Central service on 30 March 2018. Daisy Hill station is located on the fringe of Westhoughton and has seen increased patronage in recent years due to new housing developments. It is located on the 1888 route from Crow Nest Junction to Salford via Swinton. The station is a typical L&Y design with a yellow-brick ticket office at street level, with steps leading to an island platform. The platform would have had waiting rooms underneath a substantial iron and glass canopy. Unfortunately, at Daisy Hill, the platform buildings and canopy were removed in the 1970s. Until 1966, the route here consisted of four tracks; the site of the pair 'fast lines' that avoided all the stations are on the extreme left of this scene.

Class 142 Pacers 142005 and 142009 were stood at Swinton while working the 14.19 Blackburn to Southport service on 18 September 2018. This service would take a circuitous 74-mile route from East Lancashire via Todmorden, traversing part of the Calder Valley main line to Manchester Victoria, then onwards, taking the Wigan route at Windsor Bridge North Junction just beyond the station at Salford Crescent. The station at Swinton has retained its former Lancashire and Yorkshire Railway platform canopy. The site of the pair of fast lines was located to the right of the Class 142s.

The station at Walkden is located on an embankment and is close to the busy shopping centre that is straddled along the A6 trunk road. Walkden has retained its L&Y platform canopy, providing passengers with some protection from the elements. Getting underway, Class 142 142033 was bringing up the rear of the 11.19 Blackburn to Southport service on 16 August 2018.

Recently transferred to Northern and in de-branded First Great Western livery, Class 150/1 Sprinter 150122 was passing Ince with the 13.23 Southport to Manchester Airport service on 23 February 2018. Ince is located just over 1 mile east of Wigan Wallgate. The route along here once had four tracks.

In the fading light of a Summer evening, a six-car BRCW Class 104 'White Line' DMU formation was arriving at Wigan Wallgate with a Manchester Victoria to Southport service on 26 August 1977. The leading car was Driving Motor Brake Second (DMBS) M50472. The Newton Heath-allocated white liners were normally associated with the Manchester Victoria to Blackpool North services but also had certain workings on the Southport line. In 1977, the original Lancashire and Yorkshire Railway island platform buildings with their iron and glass platform canopy, gas lights, and BR 1950s maroon enamel signage were still in existence at Wigan Wallgate and provided a time warp experience on a rapidly changing BR network. Wallgate was in complete contrast to the bare windswept 1970s modernity at nearby Wigan North Western, which was brutally rebuilt as a precursor to the electrification of the WCML.

In its obsolete EWS livery, Class 66 66142 had just passed under the WCML and was running through Wigan Wallgate with the 10.50 Knowsley to Wilton binliner service on 20 April 2018. The service moves containerised non-recyclable rubbish from Merseyside, which is incinerated at Teesside to generate electricity and provide thermal energy to firms around the Wilton International Business Site. Wigan Wallgate has a single-island platform with a west-facing bay platform for terminating services from Southport and Kirkby. The bay is also used to stable diesel units overnight.

A view across the disused small goods yard at Wigan Wallgate on the evening of 10 September 1977 as Class 86 86236 was approaching Wigan North Western at speed with a southbound express made up of Mk 1, Mk 2, and Mk 3 stock. The Class 86 was then unnamed; in 1980, it would be christened *Josiah Wedgwood Master Potter 1736–1795*. In the foreground is one of British Leyland's finest—the then two-year-old Morris Marina 1.3 will now be long gone. Similarly, but after a much longer life, 86236 was scrapped in 2003, in the period when such fine locomotives were being ousted in favour of new Virgin Voyagers and Pendolinos.

Having last called at Wigan North Western, Virgin Pendolino 390122 was accelerating past the depot at Wigan Springs Branch while working the 12.45 Carlisle to London Euston service (1M12) on 28 April 2018. The junction of the route to Liverpool via St Helens Central is just visible on the extreme left towards the rear of the train. The former diesel depot at Springs Branch has been used by Network Rail for many years is now a Northern Rail stabling facility for Electric Multiple Units.

Having just passed through Wigan Wallgate, Class 66 66171 was passing over the busy A49 Southgate and the River Douglas with the 07.25 Wilton to Knowsley empty binliner service on 24 July 2018. The concrete overbridge was a replacement for the original 1848 Liverpool and Bury Railway structure. Replaced in 1947, it was the first railway bridge in the UK to be constructed from pre-stressed concrete beams. Designed by the LMS Chief Civil Engineer William Kelly Wallace, the beams had originally been prepared in 1939 for wartime use to replace damaged bridge spans as necessary.

On what was once the Lancashire and Yorkshire main line between Wigan Wallgate and Liverpool Exchange, former First Great Western Class 150/1 150125 had just passed under the substantial stone bridge that takes the A571 Billinge Road over the line as it arrived at Pemberton while working the 13.44 Kirkby to Blackburn, via Manchester Victoria service on 13 April 2018. The station at Pemberton was once adjacent to a large colliery complex complete with coke ovens. It was all closed in 1970, and the area is now landscaped.

In newly applied Northern livery, Class 150/2 Sprinter 150276 was arriving at Orrell with the 10.44 Kirkby to Blackburn service on 6 April 2018. Orrell is a small town that is close to both the M6 and M58 motorways.

Above left: On the Southport to Wigan Wallgate route, Class 142s 142056 and 142001 were approaching the small station at Appley Bridge with the 14.51 Southport to Manchester Victoria service on 4 June 2016. Now a quiet residential village, Appley Bridge once had a busy industrial past. Located close to the Leeds and Liverpool Canal, there were once paint and linoleum factories, quarries, and clay pits for local brickworks.

Above right: In Northern liveries old and new, Class 153 and Class 150/1 153359 and 150138 were arriving at Bromley Cross with the 16.18 Blackburn to Rochdale service on 25 July 2018. The signal box just visible to the right of the 153 is a fringe box to both the power boxes at Manchester Piccadilly and Preston. The signal box was built in 1875 by the Manchester company Smith and Yardley, and it once controlled a level crossing sited at the end of the station platforms. Now a foot crossing only, it was closed to vehicular traffic in 1966. Located on the Ribble Valley route from Blackburn, Bromley Cross is on the northernmost boundary of the Greater Manchester network.

Class 153 153328 and Class 150/1 150115 were crossing the A58 Compton Way as they were departing from Hall 'i th Wood with the 09.25 Clitheroe to Manchester Victoria service on 20 May 2018. The station here has staggered platforms either side of the substantial bridge and was opened on 29 September 1986. It is the last station on the Ribble Valley line before Bolton. Hall 'i th Wood refers to the nearby sixteenth-century Grade I-listed manor house, made famous by the inventor Samuel Crompton, who in 1779 designed and built the world's first 'Spinning Mule', one of the many pioneers of the once great Lancashire cotton industry.

Class 142 142046 was passing over Croal Viaduct on the exit from Bolton while working the 12.45 Manchester Victoria to Clitheroe service on 20 May 2018. The viaduct spans the River Croal, the abandoned course of the Manchester, Bolton, and Bury Canal, as well as the A673 and A666. Now just carrying a single track, the viaduct consists of four cast iron spans, each with a width of 76 feet, plus six stone arches that are each 36 feet across. Built by the Bolton and Blackburn Railway in 1847, the supervising engineer was Charles Vignoles. The segmented iron spans were cast in Preston at the foundry of Ogle, Son and Co. Among other items the foundry produced was the ironwork for the Winter Gardens complex in Blackpool.

On a grey, cold, and damp winter day, with the town hall clock tower dominating the skyline, DRS Class 47 47818 was arriving at Bolton with the 12.47 Buckshaw Parkway to Manchester Victoria 'Christmas Shoppex' service on 6 December 2014. With the loco and coaches provided by direct rail services to Northern Rail, these loco-hauled services ran on pre-Christmas Saturdays to increase capacity along this well-patronised route.

The driver was looking back as passengers alighted and boarded Cravens Class 105 Driving Motor Brake Second M50755, as it was stood at Bolton as the lead car of a Kirkby–Wigan Wallgate–Manchester Victoria service on 23 June 1979. The Sheffield-built Cravens Power Twin fleet based at Newton Heath Depot were a joy to behold; they were rundown and noisy but with well-sprung seats and a warm interior that smelled of diesel fuel. The degree of rattle from the metal interior fittings was dependent on engine revs and speed, and it was all topped off with an interior that had 1950s green Formica panels.

Due to engineering work on the WCML between Crewe and Preston, services were diverted via Manchester and Bolton for several weekends in the late autumn of 2003. Virgin Trains Class 87 87021 *Robert the Bruce* was trailing at the rear of the diesel hauled 08.56 London Euston to Glasgow Central service (1S67), passing through Bolton on 1 November 2003. Originally known as Bolton Trinity Street, the station once had a pair of through tracks between the main platform roads. Since this image was recorded, the trackless platform on the extreme left has been brought back into use (platform 5) as part of the Preston to Manchester electrification upgrade works.

With electrification work still in progress, a pair of TransPennine Express Class 185s—185109 and 185151—were accelerating away from Bolton with the 14.48 Barrow-in-Furness to Manchester Airport service on 18 September 2018.

Class 180 180106 was about to pass through the 295-yard Farnworth Tunnel while working the 14.23 Preston to Hazel Grove service on a damp 29 August 2011. As a precursor to electrification, the tunnel was rebuilt during 2015 and only an enlarged bore carrying double track is now in use. The former Down line bore seen on the right of this view was taken out of use and is now devoid of track. Northern Rail leased three former First Great Western Alstom-built Class 180 units (180103, 106, and 109) between 2008 and 2012 to increase capacity on the busy Blackpool–Preston–Manchester corridor.

A view down the cobbled station approach road as a pair of Class 153 single units—153317 and 153304—were passing the small and unstaffed but once-busy station at Clifton while working the 11.03 Manchester Victoria to Clitheroe service on 8 April 2018. Formerly known as Clifton Junction, this was where the former East Lancashire Railway main line from Accrington and Bury met the Manchester–Bolton route. The disused platforms were on the extreme left of the approach road, with the actual junction located just beyond the signal. The Accrington route, once so busy with freight and passenger traffic on a system that buzzed with activity, was closed in December 1966. The abandoned platforms are still there in the trees. There was also a former LNWR line from Patricroft on the Liverpool to Manchester route, that had a junction at Clifton, but this ceased to be a through route following the collapse of Clifton Hall Tunnel at Swinton in 1953. Renamed in 1974, Clifton station is now only served by two trains daily, its passenger usage in the period 2016–17 was just 352.

Above left: Pioneer Class 142 142001 was leading the 11.05 Southport to Hazel Grove service past Brindle Heath on 8 April 2018. In the background is the rail-served Greater Manchester Waste Disposal Authority facility. To the right of the 142, alongside the fence, was once the course of the Manchester, Bolton, and Bury Canal.

Above right: First TransPennine Express Class 185 185103 was threading through the industrial landscape of Pendlebury on its way to its next call at Salford Crescent with the 10.23 Barrow-in-Furness to Manchester Airport service on 8 April 2018. The remains of Kingston Mill located on nearby Cobden Street and dating from 1891 dominate the backdrop, while on the extreme left alongside the fence was once the course of the long-abandoned Manchester, Bolton, and Bury Canal. Opening in 1808, the canal finally closed in 1961; the section from Agecroft to Salford has virtually disappeared from the landscape. The artist L. S. Lowry resided in Pendlebury from 1909 to 1948.

With the former Manchester Corporation Electricity Works as a backdrop, Freightliner Class 66 66563 was passing through Windsor Bridge North Junction on the approach to Salford Crescent with the 15.46 Brindle Heath to Dean Lane containerised refuse service on 18 September 2018. The train is running on the route from Bolton, while the tracks bearing towards the left are the 1888 route via Swinton, to Crow Nest Junction at Hindley near Wigan.

With the station lights still lit on an overcast June morning, a solitary passenger watches Freightliner Class 66 66607 passing through Salford Crescent with the 07.51 Pendleton Brindle Heath to Tunstead Sidings aggregate empties on 11 June 2016. The single-island platform at Salford Crescent is a busy location. Opened in 1988 commensurate with the Windsor Link that enabled services from the north to run to Manchester Piccadilly, the station has become an interchange for services for both Victoria and Piccadilly stations. Salford Crescent is adjacent to Salford University and the busy A6 trunk road.

Bringing a welcome sight at a location that is dominated by Diesel Multiple Units, DB Cargo Class 66 66145 in obsolete EWS livery, was passing over Windsor Bridge South Junction on the approach to Salford Crescent while working the 07.25 Wilton to Knowsley binliner on 21 August 2018. Windsor Bridge South Junction is the divergence of the Windsor Link, that takes services South towards Ordsall Lane Junction, Deansgate, Oxford Road, and Piccadilly.

2

East and North-East

At what is now the headquarters of the preserved East Lancashire Railway, a 1,200-V DC Class 504 EMU, with Driving Trailer M77173 leading, was awaiting departure from Bury Bolton Street with a service to Manchester Victoria on 28 May 1979. The station here was once on the East Lancashire Railway route to Accrington, Rawtenstall, and Bacup. The Accrington and Bacup lines were closed in 1966 and the Rawtenstall passenger services were withdrawn in 1972. In 1979, beyond Bury, only a weekly coal train ran to the terminus at Rawtenstall. This service finally ceased operation in December 1980. Bury Bolton Street station was closed on 17 March 1980, all services being transferred to the new Bury Interchange station.

Bury Interchange was opened in March 1980 and was located close to the famous Bury Market, the town centre, and the bus station. It was a functional design, located below street level, constructed in concrete and brick; it was used by the BR Manchester to Bury electric services until 1991. The line from Bury to Manchester was converted to be the first section of the Manchester Metrolink system, opening for business in April 1992. On 27 April 1991, with only a few months of operation left, a Class 504 set (M77180 and M65459) was departing from Bury Interchange with a service to Manchester Victoria. Carrying the corporate GM livery, the Class 504 units were subject to graffiti attacks during their last stint of operation. In the foreground of this scene is the abandoned flat crossing, which was once the site of the large Bury Knowsley Street station, the remaining single line being used until December 1980 for the remaining coal trains running from Heywood to Rawtenstall.

The 8.5-mile Manchester to Bury line was originally electrified by the Lancashire and Yorkshire Railway in 1916, using a side-contact current collection system. It was a busy route that carried heavy commuter and residential traffic. The original electric sets were replaced by twenty-six two-car Class 504 EMUs, built at Wolverton Works in 1959. The fleet carried a variety of liveries during their thirty-two years of operation; during the 1970s, the operational sets were finished in BR Rail Blue with the Greater Manchester 'M' logo alongside the BR emblems. On 15 May 1979, several sets were stabled at Bury Electric Depot.

The preserved East Lancashire Railway was opened in three stages—Bury to Ramsbottom in 1987, Ramsbottom to Rawtenstall in 1991, and from Bury to Heywood in 2003—giving a route mileage of 12.5 miles. At Castleton, beyond Heywood, there is a connection with the national network, which enables stock and locomotive movements from various parts of the UK network. On 12 October 2013, an East Midlands HST on a charter service run from London St Pancras to Rawtenstall, making it the first time an HST had visited the line. Power car 43049 *Neville Hill TMD* was passing over the level crossing at Rawtenstall West, bringing up the rear of the train on the outward journey. The traditional wooden level crossing gates here have since been replaced with modern lifting barriers.

A pair of Class 504 EMUs with Driving Trailer M77175 leading were crossing Radcliffe Viaduct *en route* from Bury to Manchester Victoria with a peak time service on 30 September 1989. Behind the viaduct is Pioneer Cotton Mill, dating from 1905. There was once a junction at Radcliffe for the former East Lancashire Railway main line that ran from Clifton Junction on the Manchester–Bolton route. The line once enabled trains to run to Accrington via Bury and was closed in December 1966.

As the *Manchester Evening News* was being delivered to a newsagent shop at the junction of Woodlands Road and Cardinal Street, a Class 504 EMU (M77172 and M65461) was departing from Woodlands Road with a Manchester Victoria to Bury service on 7 July 1991. The distant signal is cleared for the signal ahead at nearby Crumpsall. There were just six days left of operation along here; the Manchester to Crumpsall section was closed on 13 July 1991 in preparation for conversion to the Metrolink.

With industrial buildings old and new as a backdrop, Merseyrail-liveried Class 142 142045, with First North Western branding, was stood at Shaw and Compton on the Oldham Loop with the 15.45 to Wigan Wallgate on 3 October 2002. The line was double track from Thorpes Bridge Junction at Newton Heath, but beyond Shaw and Crompton, it latterly became single track to Rochdale, where the loop joined the Calder Valley main line. Part of the former double-track formation at Shaw was kept as a turnback siding as many of the services along the loop from Manchester Victoria terminated at Shaw. The Oldham Loop closed on 3 October 2009 for conversion to the Metrolink.

Above left: The view down Heywood Street, as Northern Class 155 155347 was approaching Castleton while working the 11.08 Manchester Victoria to Leeds service on 15 May 2011. The seven former West Yorkshire PTE two-car Class 155 sets are a familiar sight along the former L&Y Calder Valley main line that connects Greater Manchester to West Yorkshire. There is a connection near the signal box on to the preserved East Lancashire Railway towards Heywood. There are plans to build an interchange station here between the national network and the ELR.

Above right: The former cotton town of Rochdale (which was originally part of Lancashire) was the birthplace of the cooperative movement founded in 1844; the hometown of the singer, entertainer, and film star Gracie Fields (1898–1979); and has probably the finest Victorian Gothic Revival town hall in the UK, reflecting the wealth of the town during the industrial revolution, when Rochdale was recognised as one of the first industrial towns. The station once had an extensive layout with a pair of island platforms, underneath a lofty iron and glass overall roof, but the facilities are now reduced to one single-island platform with an east-facing bay. Northern Class 142 142041 was departing with the 10.44 Kirkby to Blackburn service on 23 August 2016. Since 2014, the Metrolink has run behind the brick wall on the left of this scene.

Freightliner Class 66 66523 was about to bear down upon the small station at Smithy Bridge while working the 09.11 Redcar to Fiddlers Ferry Power Station on 6 April 2018. Formed of HHA bogie hopper wagons, the service was moving coal stocks from the closed Redcar Steelworks to the Power Station at Fiddlers Ferry near Warrington. The station at Smithy Bridge on the former L&Y Calder Valley main line was opened in August 1985 and was a replacement for the original station that had been closed in 1960.

The seven Northern Rail Class 155s are regular performers on the Calder Valley route between Leeds and Manchester Victoria. No. 155342 was passing over the original 1839 Manchester and Leeds Railway stone viaduct as it prepared to call at Littleborough while working the 09.37 Leeds to Manchester Victoria service on 12 May 2012. Below the train is Canal Street, a reminder that the nearby Rochdale Canal was the first trans-Pennine route here, opening in 1804.

With traffic queuing on Oldham Road and commuters making their way from the station, Class 142 142023 was departing from Mills Hill with the 14.25 Clitheroe to Rochdale service on 21 August 2018. The small station here was opened in 1985 and serves Middleton and Chadderton.

At the market town of Glossop in High Peak, Derbyshire, Class 305 EMU 305507 (in newly applied BR Regional Railways livery) arrived with a service from Hadfield on 28 February 1992. Following reversal at Glossop, the 305 was heading for Manchester Piccadilly via Dinting. The services were originally worked by Class 506s until the line was re-engineered from 1,500-V DC to 25-Kv AC in December 1984, when Class 304/305 units and some ex-Glasgow Class 303s worked on the Manchester–Glossop–Hadfield services until the introduction of the new Hunslet-built Class 323 EMUs in 1994. The short 1-mile Glossop Branch from Dinting was electrified as part of the Manchester–Sheffield 'Woodhead' electrification scheme in 1954.

In the Regional Railways/Greater Manchester livery, Class 305 305515 was crossing on to the single-track Glossop Branch as it arrived at Dinting with a Manchester Piccadilly–Glossop–Hadfield service on 13 September 1997. The single line to the right was once part of the Manchester–Sheffield Woodhead main line. There is a triangular layout at Dinting, and a handful of peak time trains run direct to and from Hadfield without calling at Glossop.

Most services to Hadfield run via Glossop, using platform 2 at Dinting. However, during the morning and evening peak, several services run direct from Hadfield and do not call at Glossop; these services utilise the one surviving former Woodhead main line platform at Dinting (platform 1). Having run the mile from the terminus at Hadfield, Class 323 323229 was arriving at Dinting with the 17.08 Hadfield to Manchester Piccadilly service on 11 September 2018. The former Great Central Railway signal box controls the triangular layout here, as well as the remaining signals on the Glossop and Hadfield single lines.

The sharply curved platform 2 at Dinting was playing host to Class 305 305510 with a Hadfield–Glossop–Manchester Piccadilly service on 13 September 1997. Restricted clearances here prevented the use of new Class 323 EMUs until the track was realigned.

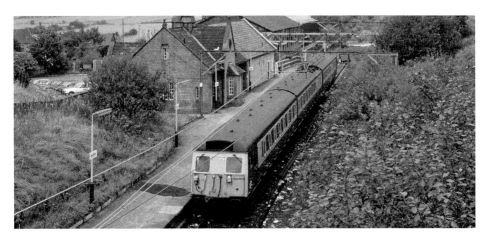

Class 304 304029 was stood on what was once the Up Line to Sheffield, while stood at Hadfield, having arrived with a service from Manchester Piccadilly and Glossop on 3 February 1990. The Manchester–Sheffield Woodhead route had been electrified in 1954, and at the time of opening was the most modern main line in Britain (one of its new electric locomotives, 26020 had been exhibited at the Festival of Britain in 1951); however, following the boom of the 1950s and 1960s, a gradual decline began. Express passenger services were withdrawn between Manchester Piccadilly and Sheffield Victoria in January 1970, with the route still being busy with freight. Unfortunately, the amount of freight using the route declined in the late 1970s and total closure east of Hadfield and west of Penistone (including the 3-mile 'New' Woodhead Tunnel under the Pennines) occurred on 18 July 1981—how the mighty fall.

With the Glossop Community Allotments as a foreground, 323230 was passing over Dinting Viaduct on the approach to its next call at Dinting with the 11.48 Manchester Piccadilly to Hadfield (via Glossop) on 25 March 2018. The 14-mile run to the terminus at Hadfield, via a reversal at Glossop, would see the 323 call at eight intermediate stations and take around thirty-eight minutes to complete its journey. This section of railway was once the 'main line' of the Woodhead route connecting Manchester with Sheffield. Opened in 1844 by the Sheffield, Ashton-under-Lyne and Manchester Railway, Dinting Viaduct is 119 feet high and originally had timber arches. These were replaced by iron girders in 1859, and seven additional brick piers were added to the 1,200-foot-long structure between 1918 and 1920.

One of the original 1,500-V DC Class 506 EMUs (with Driving Trailer M59603M leading) was arriving at Godley Junction with a Hadfield–Glossop–Manchester Piccadilly service on 29 November 1984. There were eight of these LNER-designed three-car EMUs introduced in 1954; they plied their daily trade until 7 December 1984, when the line temporarily closed prior to being re-electrified using the standard 25-Kv AC system. The services were then operated by Class 303, 304, and 305 EMUs until the new Hunslet-built Class 323 fleet was delivered in 1990s. The station at Godley Junction has also passed into history; it closed in May 1995.

Sunlight and shade at Guide Bridge on 10 September 1979. Class 76 76009 had emerged from the stabling sidings at the south end of the station and was preparing to take over a diesel-hauled freight for the run over the Pennines to Sheffield. Everything in this image has since been lost. This side of the station has now been cleared and forms part of the station car park. The Tommy (Class 76 loco) was new from nearby Gorton Works in March 1951 as 26009, and, along with nine other early built locos, it was trialled on the 1,500-V DC system in Essex during 1951. Following the trials, they all migrated north in June 1951 for further trials and testing as some short sections of the Woodhead system had been energised prior to completion of the scheme. The loco lasted the full term of service on the Woodhead route from full opening in 1954 until it closed in July 1981, with 76009 clocking up just over thirty years of service. After the line closed, it spent some time stored along with other surviving Tommies at Reddish Depot, until it made one last journey to Sheffield (Diesel hauled via the Hope Valley) and was scrapped in July 1983 by Booth's of Rotherham.

TransPennine Express Class 185 185115 was passing through Guide Bridge with the 12.16 Manchester Airport to York service (1P32) on 16 August 2016. Including a reversal at Manchester Piccadilly, the 185 would complete its 79-mile journey over the Pennines via Stalybridge and Huddersfield in one hour and thirty-four minutes.

Class 323 323224 was arriving at Hattersley with the 09.29 Hadfield–Glossop–Manchester Piccadilly service on 5 May 2018. Hattersley in Tameside is 9 miles out from Piccadilly, and the station with a single-island platform was opened by BR in 1978. The 323 has just run through a cutting that was once part of a tunnel. The two Hattersley tunnels were 'opened out' by the LNER between 1927 and 1930.

Class 142 142009 was passing through the small unstaffed station at Hyde North with the 10.34 Manchester Piccadilly to Rose Hill Marple service on 5 May 2018. Until 1951, the station was called Hyde Junction but has only ever had platforms on the branch. In the background is the electrified Piccadilly to Glossop and Hadfield (former Woodhead) route, while the 142 is running along what was the joint Midland and Great Central line towards Romiley.

Class 323 323228 was stood at Ashburys with the 13.18 Manchester Piccadilly to Hadfield via Glossop service on 16 August 2016. Beyond the platforms is Ashburys West Junction, a useful connection to Philips Park Junction that enables freight, engineers working, and empty stock movements to access the Manchester Victoria to Rochdale route at Miles Platting.

The penultimate Siemens-built Class 185, 185150 was passing the single, little-used island platform at Ardwick with the TransPennine Express 12.33 Manchester Airport to York service on 3 April 2016. On the extreme left of this scene are the busy Manchester Piccadilly to Crewe lines. Ardwick is located on the former Great Central route that was once part of the Manchester–Sheffield line. The small station is in a non-residential area about 1 mile from Manchester Piccadilly. There are only two timetabled trains that call at Ardwick at peak times in each direction on a Monday–Friday. The footfall at this urban out-of-the-way station for the period 2016–17 was just 850.

Running under what was then 1,500-V DC catenary, Class 25s 25057 and 25083 were taking the Great Central route at Ardwick while working the LCGB 'The Easter Tommy' railtour on 21 April 1981. The pair of Class 25s would be exchanged for a Class 76 electric loco 76025 at Guide Bridge, for the run to Sheffield via Woodhead. The train would be the last locomotive hauled passenger train to traverse the Manchester–Sheffield main line in both directions. The Class 08 shunter was stood where there is now a TransPennine Express depot and servicing facility.

With the Pennines on the horizon, Class 185 185108 was running below the rear of the houses on Manchester Road as it was passing Mossley with the 12.17 Newcastle to Manchester Airport TransPennine Express service (1P26) on 10 June 2018. The 185 is traversing what was once the LNWR Leeds to Manchester main line.

On the east side of Manchester at the foot of the Pennines, Stalybridge was once the meeting point of three pre-grouping railway companies—the L&Y, LNWR, and Great Central. The station had a major upgrade, completed in 2012, but the original buildings on the Up platform were retained and are the home of an award-winning buffet and bar. In the days when express services over the former LNWR route to Huddersfield and Leeds were loco-hauled, a scruffy looking Class 47 47631 was stood at Stalybridge with the 12.52 Liverpool Lime Street to Newcastle service formed of Mk 2 stock on 24 March 1990.

Northern Class 156 156452 was arriving at Ashton-under-Lyne with the 10.21 Blackpool North to Huddersfield service on 19 March 2016. The bracketed distant signal on the Down Line was controlled by the then extant signal box at nearby Ashton Moss North Junction.

Ashton Moss North Junction is where the former LNWR Manchester–Huddersfield–Leeds main line has a junction with the route to Stockport via Denton. The junction here was remodelled and the signal box abolished in April 2018. Looking very much like a model railway that has newly laid track and pristine ballast, TransPennine Express Class 185 185115 was passing over the junction while working the 07.17 York to Manchester Airport service on 10 June 2018.

Above left: Class 142s 142034 and 142048 were departing from Reddish South with the once-weekly Friday only 'Parliamentary' 09.22 Stockport to Stalybridge service on 30 March 2018. Running from Heaton Norris Junction, just north of Stockport, through to Guide Bridge, the now single-track route only had one timetabled passenger train in one direction, once a week. The footfall for 2016–17 here was just ninety-four passengers. The service also called at nearby Denton. At Denton, there is a junction that leads to Ashton Moss North Junction on the Manchester–Ashton-under-Lyne route; consequently, the line through Denton and Reddish South sees some freight and empty stock activity on a daily basis.

Above right: Freightliner Class 66 66563 was stood in the Greater Manchester Waste Disposal Authority yard at Reliance Street, while Metrolink M5000 3010 was passing by with a Rochdale via Oldham service on 21 August 2018. The 66 had worked in with the 15.46 Brindle Heath to Dean Lane and was being unloaded and reloaded for the return journey across Manchester back to Brindle Heath. The double-track line here was once part of the Oldham Loop. The non-electrified track is the access from nearby Thorpes Bridge Junction at Newton Heath to the waste facility. The other electrified track is now used exclusively by the Metrolink, and this section is bi-directional.

Below: The Lancashire and Yorkshire Railway opened a large locomotive depot at Newton Heath in 1876. It was located just over two miles east of Manchester Victoria and was in the V-shape of Thorpes Bridge Junction, where the Oldham Loop diverged from the Calder Valley main line. The depot always had a large allocation of steam locomotives, but DMUs were part of the scene at Newton Heath from the late 1950s. The depot was closed to steam in April 1968; since then, it has become the main maintenance and berthing facility for Northern Rail diesel units in the Manchester and north-west area. Under a threatening sky, 142003, 142035, and 153317 were stabled in the depot yard on 16 September 2007. All three units are in the then obsolete First North Western livery and with the first style temporary 'Northern' branding.

3

City Environs

In the consist of a freight train bound for Horwich Works, Southern Region vintage 4-SUB EMU 4647 was at the rear, gingerly descending the 1-in-55 gradient of Miles Platting bank as it arrived at Manchester Victoria on 16 September 1980. Note the staff in the signal box at Victoria East Junction looking on at this not too familiar sight. 4647, which was heading for scrapping at Horwich, had been built by BR in 1951 to a pre-war Southern Railway design.

With the architectural splendour of Manchester Victoria East Junction signal box as a backdrop, Class 45 45035 was stabled between duties on 16 September 1980. Looking as though it was designed by a committee with a grudge, the signal box dated from 1962 and was fitted with a Westinghouse switch panel. It closed in 1998 when control passed to the Manchester North Signalling Centre at Salford Crescent, and the structure has since been demolished.

Complete with its first-class saloon and a paraffin tail lamp, Class 110 Driving Motor Composite Lavatory Car (DMCL) E52081 was at the rear of a Manchester Victoria to Leeds service on 28 September 1979. Fitted with 180-hp Rolls-Royce engines, the BRCW Class 110 three-car units (dating from 1961) had the highest power-to-weight ratio of the BR first generation DMU fleet. They were synonymous with the steeply graded former Lancashire and Yorkshire Railway Calder Valley main line between Manchester, Bradford Exchange, and Leeds.

Above: With only pigeons for company, a Manchester to Bury Class 504 EMU formed of cars M65452 and M77173 was stood at platform 5 at Manchester Victoria on 5 March 1979. The terminal platforms still had BR 1950s maroon enamel signage. This side of Victoria has since been radically remodelled and has a new roof to accommodate the busy and expanded Metrolink system.

Right: In the Manchester Victoria of old, Class 45 45143 was stood at platform 12 with the 16.05 Liverpool Lime Street to Newcastle service on 12 June 1979. The boarding passengers silhouetted in the background have almost a Lowry-like gait. Just out of sight to the right was the BR Travellers Fare buffet, 'The Coastal', which was then a popular watering hole, serving typical 1970s fare that would not pass muster these days. On the extreme left is part of what was once the longest station platform in the UK. Platform 11 connected Victoria and Exchange stations and was 2,238 feet (682 m) in length; it could accommodate three trains. The image sums up Manchester Victoria at the time—tatty, dirty, oil-soaked tracks, and rundown, with a hotchpotch of buildings and canopies, yet full of character and interest. Victoria was badly damaged during the Manchester Blitz in December 1940, when most of the overall roof over the through platforms was destroyed, never to be replaced, giving this section a 'patched-up' appearance until it was rebuilt in 1992–1994.

In Greater Manchester livery, Class 142 142009 was stabled in the Wallside siding at Manchester Victoria on 3 February 1990. The siding was where banking engines would once be stabled to assist heavy freights up the 1-in-55 gradient of Miles Platting bank that commences just beyond the east end of the station platforms. No. 142009 was part of the batch of the first fourteen Class 142s (142001–142014) that were finished in GM colours and went new to nearby Newton Heath Depot in 1985.

Class 60 60082 with Transrail branding was approaching Manchester Victoria with Salford Hope Street to Peak Forest empty aggregate working on 24 September 2004. The track layout was simplified and realigned at the west end of Victoria following the station rebuilding in the mid-1990s. The footbridge on the left was once part of the LNWR Exchange station complex that closed in 1969. In the distance is the former Threlfall Brewery (with its brick chimney) at Cook Street, Salford. High-rise apartment buildings now dominate the skyline here.

Electric services commenced running between Liverpool Lime Street and Manchester Victoria in 2015. In a scene that is barely recognisable from days of old, Northern Electrics Class 319 319371 was arriving ECS (5F21) the short distance from the west facing reversing siding into platform 4 at Victoria, ready to form the 15.02 departure to Liverpool Lime Street on 23 August 2016.

The changing skyline of Manchester. In its revised Northern livery, Class 319 319363 was threading its way out of Victoria and approaching Salford Central with the 14.00 service to Liverpool Lime Street on 20 April 2018. The top of the brick chimney of the former Threlfall Brewery (now part of a business centre) is just visible in the upper left of this scene.

Class 150s meet at Salford Central on 20 April 2018. On the left, 150146 was arriving with the 11.45 Wigan North Western to Manchester Victoria service, while 150268 was departing with the 12.28 Manchester Victoria to Blackburn service. In an ever-changing backdrop, the small ornate building in the middle distance is the Salford Cinema dating from 1912. It became 'The Rex' in 1938, closing in 1958; from 1967 until 1985, it was a bingo hall.

Complete with a dirty face, Freightliner Class 66 66610 was rounding the curve between Salford Crescent and Salford Central with the 07.51 Pendleton to Tunstead sidings aggregate empties on an overcast 6 August 2016.

Having just passed through the new Irwell Bridge Junction, where the Ordsall Chord joins the Liverpool to Manchester route, DB Cargo Class 66 66142 was bringing the 10.50 Knowsley to Wilton binliner around the sharp curve on the approach to Salford Central on 20 April 2018.

With the traffic on Trinity Way in the foreground, Northern Class 319 319363 was heading towards Salford with the 12.22 Liverpool Lime Street to Manchester Victoria service on 20 April 2018. The bridge on the left takes the Ordsall Chord over the River Irwell, the short section of line between Water Street Junction and Irwell Bridge Junction that opened in December 2017 and enables services to run between Piccadilly and Victoria.

With part of the original 1830 Liverpool and Manchester Railway station platform in the foreground, West Coast Class 47 47500 was stabled in the former Liverpool Road station on 3 February 2013. The loco had made the television news on 23 January when, at the rear of an Ardwick to Carnforth ECS move, the loco derailed and caught fire at nearby Ordsall Lane Junction. It was removed for safekeeping into the Museum of Science and Industry yard for assessment. The L&M station was opened on 15 September 1830 and was in use until 1844, when a connection was opened from Ordsall Lane to the Manchester and Leeds Railway station at Hunts Bank (Manchester Victoria). Liverpool Road then became a goods depot and was in use until 1975. Fortunately, the original buildings and ground level platform areas survived intact and are now part of the Manchester Museum of Science and Industry (MOSI) complex.

On the former Manchester South Junction and Altrincham (MSJ&A) route, a pair of East Midlands Trains Class 158s—158854 and 158873—were passing the apartment blocks at St Georges Island, Castlefield, while working the 11.52 Liverpool Lime Street to Norwich service on 25 September 2018. With the Bridgewater Canal in the foreground, the derelict lock gates mark the start of the abandoned 200-m (1-furlong) Hulme branch canal arm. Opened in 1838, the short stretch of waterway ran between the Bridgewater Canal and the nearby River Irwell. It enabled boats to run between the Manchester, Bolton, and Bury Canal at Salford via the River Irwell, gaining access to the Bridgewater and Rochdale Canals at Castlefield. The arm was in use until 1985, when a new lock from the Bridgewater Canal to the Irwell was opened at Pomona.

With traffic queuing on the A57 ring road, Northern Class 156s 156464 and 156491 were heading towards Castlefield Junction with the 12.16 Liverpool Lime Street to Manchester Airport service on 18 September 2018.

Northern Class 150/1 150146 was passing over the cast iron bridge span that crosses the Bridgewater Canal junction at Castlefield, while working the 10.19 Liverpool Lime Street to Manchester Oxford Road service on 18 September 2018. Through the arch are the basins at Potato Wharf, while out of sight to the right foreground is the start of the 32-mile Rochdale Canal. The viaduct in the background is the route from Deansgate via Castlefield Junction and connects with the Ordsall Chord at nearby Water Street and the historic (1830) Liverpool to Manchester route at Ordsall Lane Junction. The lattice girder bridge was the route to and from the former terminus at Manchester Central that closed in 1969; it is now used by the Metrolink between Deansgate-Castlefield and Cornbrook.

Manchester old and new. With Dukes Lock number ninety-two on the Rochdale Canal in the foreground and the forty-seven-storey, 554-foot (169-m) Beetham Tower dominating the skyline, GBRf Class 66 66733 *Cambridge PSB* had just passed through Castlefield Junction and was making its way along the former Manchester South Junction and Altrincham Railway viaduct at Castlefield with the 03.10 Felixstowe to Trafford Park intermodal service on 18 September 2018. From being new in 2003, until 2011, the 66 was part of the DRS fleet numbered 66401.

On a cold and damp winter day, TransPennine Express Class 350/4 350405 was passing over Deansgate and the Bridgewater Canal while working the 10.12 Edinburgh to Manchester Airport service (1M95) on 16 December 2017. Having last called at Wigan North Western and run to Manchester over Chat Moss, the next call for the 350 would be at nearby Oxford Road.

Class 304 304034 was awaiting departure from Deansgate with a Crewe service via the Styal Loop on 25 April 1992. The Class 304s were a familiar sight on South Manchester area suburban duties from their introduction in 1960 until the last well-worn examples were withdrawn in 1996.

The view along the Rochdale Canal at lock ninety at the west end of Whitworth Street West as First TransPennine Class 185 185124 was approaching Deansgate station with a Liverpool Lime Street service in 2011. The brick building in the centre of this image was once the site of the Hacienda nightclub, famous for the Manchester music scene in the 1980s and 1990s.

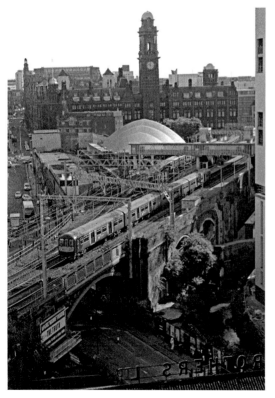

Above: Freightliner Class 70s 70011 and 70010 were passing along the viaduct that runs parallel to Whitworth Street West and its plethora of office and apartment buildings as they approached Manchester Oxford Road with the 11.17 Trafford Park Freightliner Terminal to Crewe Basford Hall service on 6 August 2016. Just visible above the rear cab roof of 70011 through the gap in the buildings is the Rochdale Canal, which opened in 1804.

Left: Northern Electrics Class 319 319363 was passing above the junction of Whitworth Street West and Cambridge Street as it departed from Manchester Oxford Road while working the 09.40 Manchester Airport to Liverpool Lime Street service on 23 August 2016. Despite the building of many high-rise apartment blocks near to Oxford Road, the distinctive 217-foot-high former Refuge Assurance office clock tower, which was completed in 1912, still dominates the skyline here.

In DB-branded EWS livery, Class 66 66172 was threading through Manchester Oxford Road with a lightly loaded 13.12 Trafford Park to London Gateway intermodal service on 11 September 2018. The station at Oxford Road was rebuilt in 1960 using laminated wood construction for some buildings and the platform canopies. The structures became English Heritage Grade II listed in 1995.

First TransPennine Express Class 185 185124 was crossing York Street on the approach to Manchester Oxford Road with a Manchester Airport to Windermere service on 1 May 2011. The railway is carried along here on a lengthy brick viaduct of the former Manchester South Junction and Altrincham Railway.

With Manchester Piccadilly in the far distance, Arriva Trains Wales Class 175 175114 was passing the UMIST buildings as it ran towards its next call at Oxford Road with the 13.36 Manchester Airport to Llandudno service on 6 August 2016. The 1-mile double-track section between Oxford Road and Piccadilly is one of the most intensively used stretches of railway in the UK.

A pigeon gets in on the act as the last built of the TPE Siemens Class 185 fleet, 185151, stands at platform 14 at Manchester Piccadilly with the 08.50 Scarborough to Liverpool Lime Street service on 25 March 2016. Platforms 13 and 14 are through platforms located on the west side of the overall roof.

On a fine autumn afternoon, Virgin Trains Class 87 87024 *Lord of the Isles* was departing from Manchester Piccadilly with the 14.30 to London Euston on 24 September 2004. This was twilight time for locomotive-hauled services on the WCML. With the new Class 390 Pendolino fleet being gradually introduced from 2001 onwards, the last Virgin Trains Class 87-hauled service was in June 2005. No. 87024 had been built at Crewe Works in April 1974; it would be withdrawn from service in May 2005 and was reduced to 80 tons of scrap metal in November 2005.

In revised Virgin Trains livery, consecutively numbered Pendolinos were stood at Manchester Piccadilly on the evening of 11 September 2018. No. 390050 was working the 18.15 to London Euston, while 390049 would follow with the 18.35 departure to Euston.

A former Glasgow 'Blue Train' Class 303, 303066, was stood at platform 10 under the overall roof at Manchester Piccadilly with a service to Alderley Edge via Stockport on 6 March 1990. Surplus to requirements on the Strathclyde network, several sets were transferred to the Manchester area in the early 1980s and worked various suburban services, including Glossop and Hadfield following the conversion of the route from DC to AC working in 1984. There had originally been ninety-one sets built by Pressed Steel at Linwood between 1959 and 1961 for use on the then newly electrified Glasgow suburban network.

On a cold winter day with a dusting of snow on the ground is the view across a maze of trackwork south of Manchester Piccadilly on 16 December 2017. TransPennine Express Class 185 185111 in its remembrance 'Victoria Cross Heroes' livery was arriving with the 07.50 Scarborough to Liverpool Lime Street, while Cross Country Voyager 221137 was departing with the 10.07 to Bristol Temple Meads, alongside Virgin Pendolino 390011, which was approaching journey's end with the 08.00 from London Euston. The multi-track 1-mile section between Piccadilly and Ardwick Junction is a very busy railway.

4

West and South-West

The WCML runs on the western boundary of the Greater Manchester area between Wigan and Parkside. Having just joined the West Coast Main Line at Golborne Junction, Class 66 66183 was heading for Wigan and St Helens with the Pathfinder Tours 'The Fiddlers Five' railtour from Westbury on 28 October 2017. From Golborne Junction, there is access on to the historic Liverpool and Manchester route, via the east and west curves at Parkside.

The Northern Hunslet-built Class 323 EMU fleet have worked South Manchester suburban services since new, during 2018, they spread their sphere of operation and have some diagrams between Manchester and Liverpool Lime Street. As passengers gathered themselves, 323237 was arriving at Patricroft with the 13.28 Liverpool Lime Street to Crewe service on 18 September 2018.

With the Pennines as a distant backdrop and the high-rise buildings at Eccles against a fearsome looking sky, TransPennine Express Class 185 185149 was roaring along the historic Liverpool and Manchester route while approaching Patricroft at speed with the 11.46 Scarborough to Liverpool Lime Street service (1F64) on 18 September 2018. In the past, Patricroft had a large amount of railway infrastructure. It was a four-platform through station, the route having fast and slow lines. There was a nearby locomotive depot (10C) that lasted until the end of steam traction in 1968, with goods sidings, yards, and a junction with the former LNWR line that ran to Clifton Junction on the Manchester–Bolton route. The locomotive builder Nasmyth, Wilson and Co. was also once based at Patricroft, producing locomotives between 1839 and 1938.

Once a four-track section of railway, the M602 motorway now runs alongside the Liverpool and Manchester Railway route between Eccles and Salford. TransPennine Express Class 185 185105 was working the 240-mile 07.10 Glasgow Central to Manchester Airport service on 30 March 2018. Most of these TPE Anglo–Scottish services utilise the Class 350/4 EMU fleet, but some services utilise Class 185 diesel units to maintain driver traction knowledge.

A remarkable one-off that is now unrepeatable. The finale of the 1980 Liverpool and Manchester Railway 150th anniversary celebrations saw the 1838-built locomotive *Lion* haul three replica L&MR coaches from Eccles to Liverpool Road station along the original route. On 14 September 1980, the ensemble was rumbling along at Cross Lane, Salford. On board were various VIPs, including the then Home Secretary, William Whitelaw. The blue Hillman Avenger contained armed police officers and shadowed the train along the site of the former slow lines. The M602 motorway now runs parallel to the railway along here.

With the Beetham Tower dominating the skyline, Arriva Trains Wales Class 175 175109 was running alongside the M602 at Salford while working the 08.54 Llandudno Junction to Manchester Airport service on 30 March 2018.

Running along the former Cheshire Lines (CLC) route, TransPennine Express 185143 was passing the small station at Flixton at speed while working the 11.22 Liverpool Lime Street to Scarborough service (1E85) on 30 March 2018.

Northern Class 156 156491 was stood at Urmston with the 11.19 Liverpool Lime Street to Manchester Oxford Road service on 11 September 2018. The facilities at Urmston station have been modernised on the Manchester-bound platform, while the original CLC buildings on the opposite side have been converted into a bar and grill.

With Tony the Tiger looking on, Class 09 diesel shunter 09002 in retro BR green livery was crossing Park Road on Trafford Park industrial estate, passing the Kellogg's factory while moving the loaded containers that would eventually form the GBRf 14.18 Trafford Park Freightliner Terminal to Felixstowe intermodal service on 4 October 2012. No. 09002 had originally been built at Darlington Works in 1959.

Northern Class 142 142095 was about to cross Ashley Road as it departed from Hale while working the 09.17 Manchester Piccadilly to Chester service on 29 August 2016. The level crossing and signalling are controlled by Deansgate Junction, but the vintage CLC signal box has been listed by English Heritage. No. 142095 was the penultimate Class 142 Pacer built in 1987.

Opposite above: GBRf Class 66 66703 *Doncaster PSB 1981–2002* was plodding through the gloom of a damp winter day, running alongside a part-frozen Bridgewater Canal at Pomona while reaching journey's end with the 03.15 Felixstowe to Trafford Park intermodal service (4M21) on 16 December 2017. The elevated Pomona tram stop on the Manchester Metrolink Eccles route is visible on the left of this scene. The road works in the lower left were the first earthworks for the Trafford Centre extension of the Metrolink, due for completion in 2020.

Opposite below: GBRf Class 66 66710 *Phil Packer BRIT* was emerging from Trafford Park Freightliner Terminal on to the former Cheshire Lines route with the 14.12 Trafford Park to Felixstowe intermodal service on 16 October 2018. On the right is the single-platform Manchester United Football Ground station. Opened in 1935, the station is adjacent to the south stand and is usually served by a Class 323 shuttle service from Manchester Oxford Road on match days only.

Having arrived at Altrincham with a service from Alderley Edge, Class 304 304045 was awaiting departure with the return working on 23 December 1991. This was twilight time for BR electric services from Manchester Piccadilly to Altrincham. The last electric trains ran the following day on Christmas Eve 1991, and the line was converted to become part of the Metrolink system, reopening in June 1992.

5

South and South-East

First-generation DMUs were gathered in the sidings at Longsight Depot on 31 August 1980. Centre stage is former Western Region Swindon Intercity Class 123 Driving Motor Corridor Second E52100. To the right is a Class 108, while on the left, a Class 104 keeps company with a Gloucester Class 100. The stylish Class 123s were the final flowering of the BR first-generation DMU fleet and entered service on the western region in 1963. They saw out their final days in the north, often running as a hybrid unit with part of a Swindon Class 124 TransPennine DMU. Longsight Depot is still active and maintains the Virgin Pendolino fleet as well as the Northern Class 323s used on the South Manchester suburban services.

Virgin Class 390 Pendolino 390125 was passing Levenshulme on the Up fast while working the 15.15 Manchester Piccadilly to London Euston on 25 March 2016. Legend has it that Dick Turpin, the famous highwayman, once frequented the Blue Belle Inn on nearby Barlow Road.

High above Stockport bus station, Northern Class 323 323226 was passing over Stockport Viaduct with the 11.04 Manchester Piccadilly to Crewe service on 16 August 2016. The twenty-two arches of Stockport Viaduct were immortalised in the paintings of L. S. Lowry; a flight of stone steps from the A6 road bridge down to the bus station is where the great man once set up his easel. The viaduct was completed in 1840 for the Manchester and Birmingham Railway and used 11 million bricks in its construction. When it opened for traffic, it was the largest railway viaduct in the world. In the 1880s, the enormous growth in traffic saw the structure doubled in width to accommodate four running lines.

With traffic hurtling along the M60 motorway, Virgin Pendolino 390039 was passing over Stockport Viaduct with the 11.15 Manchester Piccadilly to London Euston service on 16 August 2016. The M60 passes beneath two arches of the viaduct between Junction 27 and Junction 1. Through the second arch, in the distance is the distinctive 'Stockport Pyramid'. The blue glass-clad office structure was completed in 1992.

Still carrying its original BR Express livery, but with Alphaline Wales & Borders Trains branding, Class 158 158824 was arriving at Stockport with the 14.30 Manchester Piccadilly to Cardiff Central service on 13 October 2001. Just visible to the right of the 158 is the former LNWR Stockport No. 2 signal box, dating from 1890. There is another former LNWR signal box at the south end of the station (Stockport No. 1). Both have been retained by Network Rail to control the movements at this busy location.

Opening in 1909, the Styal Loop is a suburban slow line that bypasses Stockport and diverges from the Piccadilly to Crewe route at Slade Lane Junction, just north of Levenshulme; it rejoins the Crewe route at Wilmslow. The loop was the first section of the 25-Kv Manchester–Crewe electrification scheme in 1960 and was where many of the first-generation AC electric locomotives were tested. In its then newly applied Northern Electrics livery, Class 319 319378 was arriving at East Didsbury with the 13.16 Liverpool Lime Street to Manchester Airport service on 16 August 2016.

TransPennine Express Class 350/4 350405 was nearing the end of its lengthy journey as it passed through Heald Green with the 12.13 Edinburgh to Manchester Airport (1M97) service on 25 September 2018. Just south of Heald Green is a triangular junction that gives access to nearby Manchester Airport.

Coming and goings at Manchester Airport on 16 October 2018. On platform 4, TransPennine Express Class 185 185126 had arrived with the 07.57 from Middlesbrough and was having a quick turnaround before heading back to Teesside with the 10.47 departure. On the adjacent platform 3, 185107 was awaiting departure with the 10.53 service to Cleethorpes. Opened in 1993, adjacent to terminal 2, the station at Manchester Airport is located on a short spur from the Styal Loop, just south of Heald Green.

Northern Class 323 323231 was passing Cheadle Hulme North Junction with the 15.46 Manchester Piccadilly to Stoke-on-Trent service on 5 May 2018. Cheadle Hulme is where the Stoke line diverges from the Manchester–Crewe route. The well-patronised station has four platforms. Stoke-on-Trent is the southernmost limit of operation for the Northern Class 323 fleet.

In its Strathclyde (Glasgow) orange livery, Class 101 two-car DMU 101693 was stood at Hyde Central with the 12.49 Rose Hill Marple to Manchester Piccadilly service on 19 May 2001. Located on the line between Romiley and Hyde North, the station had a short surviving portion of its original Manchester, Sheffield, and Lincolnshire Railway platform canopy. The last surviving members of the Metro-Cammell Class 101 DMU fleet were concentrated at Longsight Depot, working out their last days in the South Manchester area until final withdrawal on Christmas Eve 2003.

Early morning light at Reddish North, as Northern Class 142s 142014 and 142062 were arriving with the 08.12 Marple to Manchester Piccadilly service on 30 March 2018. The station has retained its original MS&LR building on the Down side, with the former goods shed now in use with a timber merchant.

A woman and child greet the arrival of 142067 at Woodley while working the 15.09 Manchester Piccadilly to Rose Hill Marple service on 11 September 2018. The small, unstaffed station has retained its original iron lattice footbridge. Once a busy location for freight traffic, just north of here was Apethorne Junction with its line to Godley Junction on the Woodhead route, while Woodley Junction to the south saw the CLC line to Stockport diverge. A short section of this line survives to access the Greater Manchester Waste Disposal facility at nearby Bredbury.

In Strathclyde orange livery, Class 101 DMU 101691 had just passed over Romiley Junction with the 12.14 Manchester Piccadilly to Rose Hill Marple service on 12 May 2001. The former Midland Railway signal box controlled the junction of the two routes from Ashburys via Brinnington, and from Hyde North via Woodley. There was once a third line that diverged here, to Stockport Tiviot Dale, but that was closed in 1967. Built in 1899, the signal box at Romiley was closed in July 2015 when control of the area passed to the ROC at Ashburys. The signal box has not been demolished and has been surveyed by Historic England.

On the Manchester to Sheffield Hope Valley route, Marple is 9 miles out from Piccadilly. It is the southern limit of Manchester suburban workings and there is a turnback facility here. Having crossed from the Up to the Down Line ready for the return journey, a worn-looking Class 101 DMU, 101683, in Regional Railways livery was awaiting departure with the 15.38 Marple to Manchester Piccadilly service on 12 May 2001.

Opposite above: High above the River Goyt, de-branded First Great Western Class 150/1 150121 was approaching Marple Wharf Junction while working the 13.49 Manchester Piccadilly to Sheffield service on 13 November 2018. The 150 was passing over Marple Viaduct, constructed by the Manchester, Sheffield, and Lincolnshire Railway and opened in 1863. It has twelve stone arches and one cast iron one spanning over the canal. In the foreground is Marple Aqueduct, which carries the Peak Forest Canal 100 feet above the River Goyt. Construction commenced in 1795 and the stone structure was completed in 1800. Designed by Benjamin Outram, it is the highest masonry arch aqueduct in the UK.

Opposite below: Having run the 13 miles from Manchester Piccadilly, 142005 in Greater Manchester livery (branded 'First North Western') was stood at the single-track terminus at Rose Hill Marple, awaiting departure with the 14.49 to Piccadilly on 12 May 2001. Rose Hill was once a through station on the double-track route from Marple Wharf Junction to Macclesfield. The former North Staffordshire Railway and Manchester Sheffield and Lincolnshire Railway joint route was closed west of Rose Hill in January 1970. With a park and ride facility located behind the platform, the small station is staffed during the mornings Monday–Friday.

DB Schenker Class 66 66101 was coming off the Hazel Grove Chord with the 09.10 Peak Forest Cemex Sidings to Hope Street aggregate working on 11 June 2016. The stone was being transported in former HHA bogie Coal hopper wagons. With the tracks to Buxton just visible on the right, the Hazel Grove Chord was opened in 1986 to give better access to the Hope Valley route for trains from Manchester Piccadilly.

Metrolink: An Overview

On the opening day of the first section of the Metrolink, 6 April 1992, over what was formerly the BR Bury–Manchester Victoria line, T68 1006 was stood at Manchester Victoria following arrival from Bury. Initially, there were twenty-six (1001–1026) of the Italian-built AnsaldoBreda trams that would operate the first stages of the 750-V DC system (Bury, Piccadilly, and Altrincham).

T68 1007 was arriving at Bury Interchange at the conclusion of its journey from Piccadilly on 22 January 2012. The station at Bury was opened in 1980 and was used by the BR Manchester–Bury Class 504 electrics until 1991.

The unique yellow-and-silver-liveried T68, 1003, was trailing at the rear of an Altrincham–Bury service as it passed over Spring Lane while departing from Radcliffe on 5 January 2013.

Bombardier M5000 3022 *Spirit of Manchester*, in its special 'Manchester Bee' livery, was passing over the M60 Motorway at Junction 17 (Whitefield), as it was approaching Besses o' th' Barn, while *en route* to Bury on 25 March 2018. The unique three-layer box girder bridge that takes the Metrolink over the M60 and Bury Old Road was constructed in 1968. M5000 fleet No. 3022 commemorates the twenty-two lives lost in the atrocity at the Manchester Arena on 22 May 2017. It carries special 'Bee' decals, the worker bee being a symbol of Manchester and a sign of unity across the area following the attack.

When the Metrolink opened, the depot that included the maintenance facilities, control room, and stabling sidings were built at Queens Road, Cheetham Hill. Located alongside the Bury route, the depot also had a minuscule staff halt. On the early morning of 15 May 2011, following overnight stabling, T68s 1019 and 1026 were waiting to leave the depot complex, while 1020 was stood at the adjacent staff halt with a service to Bury. With an expanding network and a large fleet of newer M5000 vehicles, a new depot was opened at Old Trafford in 2011. The control room (Network Management Centre) was subsequently moved from Queens Road to Trafford Depot in 2013. A new stop (Queens Road) was opened on the site of the staff halt in December 2013.

The Metrolink has two service vehicles kept at Queens Road Depot. They are numbered 1027 and 1028 (in sequence with the original T68s 1001–1026). Built in 1991 by RFS Industries, 1027 has a Caterpillar 3306 PCT 170-Kw diesel engine and is also fitted with a hydraulic crane. Its support wagon, 1028, can carry various items as necessary and has been used with a scissor lift access platform for bridge and overhead line inspection and repairs.

Running into Manchester Victoria across the site of the old Bury line terminal platforms, the Metrolink takes a 90-degree turn alongside the station concourse before passing through a 'hole in the wall', which takes the system on to the city centre street-running section. On 1 May 2011, T68 1018 was about to cross Corporation Street on the exit from Victoria with a Bury–Piccadilly service.

With the need to accommodate services from Ashton, Bury, Oldham, Rochdale, and the second city crossing, the Metrolink facilities at Victoria are now much expanded and it is a very busy location. Underneath the new roof, a pair of Bombardier M5000 trams were making their way to and from the second city crossing on 21 August 2018. On the left, 3102 was on its way to Rochdale via Oldham, while running in the opposite direction, 3086 was bound for East Didsbury via Exchange Square. The stairway above the front of 3086 is the entrance to the Manchester Arena that is located above the through platforms.

M5000 3080 bound for East Didsbury was heading along Corporation Street on 21 August 2018. The route along here is the second city crossing that opened in 2017.

On the original city centre street-running section that opened in 1992, M5000 3081 was descending along Balloon Street from Shudehill on the approach to the junction with Corporation Street and Victoria station on 21 August 2018.

On a damp winter evening, T68 1017 was stood at Piccadilly Gardens with a Bury–Piccadilly station service on 26 November 2013. The Metrolink stop is located next to the adjacent bus station.

Having emerged from the undercroft terminus below Piccadilly station, T68 1010 was running alongside London Road (The old A6) with a service for Bury on 29 May 2011.

With the former Manchester Central terminus as a backdrop, traffic was waiting at the junction of Great Bridgewater Street and Lower Moseley Street, as M5000 3078 awaited the short hop to Deansgate-Castlefield to form a service to MediaCityUK on 23 August 2016. No. 3078 was one of four Metrolink M5000s that carried rainbow livery in conjunction with the Manchester Pride event to be held on the August bank holiday weekend. The National Express coach (Volvo B9R Plaxton Elite, KSK 953) is a reminder that Lower Moseley Street in the shadow of Manchester Central was once the site of the busy Lower Moseley Street bus and coach station that handled long-distance operators and was in business from 1928 until 1972.

A nocturnal scene at Deansgate-Castlefield on 26 November 2013 as T68 1017 was stood with an Eccles–MediaCityUK–Piccadilly service. The tracks here are on the site of the heavy rail lines that once served the nearby Manchester Central terminus. The Metrolink utilises the trackbed of the former Cheshire Lines route as far as Cornbrook.

High above the Bridgewater Canal, M5000s 3005 and 3009 were passing Castlefield *en route* for Altrincham on 18 September 2018. The Metrolink runs parallel with the CLC Manchester–Liverpool route between Castlefield and Pomona.

Running above the Bridgewater Canal, Manchester Metrolink M5000 3116, was passing Slate Wharf at Castlefield with a Piccadilly–MediaCityUK service on 18 September 2018. Once heavily industrialised, the area has been regenerated with canal-side residential apartment buildings.

Just west of Cornbrook is where the Manchester Airport–East Didsbury route diverges from the Eccles line. Consequently, Cornbrook is a busy interchange with frequent services. Manchester Airport services were crossing on 16 October 2018; outbound was M5000 3066, while heading for Piccadilly were 3039 and 3056.

With the pleasure boat *Princess Katherine* just visible under the bridge span, Metrolink M5000s 3110 and 3082 were crossing the Manchester Ship Canal at Pomona with an Eccles–Ashton via Piccadilly service on a damp 16 December 2017. To the left of 3110 is the course of the extension of the Metrolink to the Trafford Centre. Groundworks were taking place for the site of a short viaduct alongside Pomona Strand, which will eventually take the new line to street level to cross nearby Trafford Road.

The Eccles line threads across the redeveloped former Manchester Docks area. T68 1022 was crossing over Waterfront Quay with an Eccles–Piccadilly service on the early morning of 31 August 2013. The old dock cranes overlooking the Ontario Basin, kept as a link with the past, were unfortunately scrapped in October 2013.

With the distinctive roof architecture of the Imperial War Museum North visible on the left, T68 1002 was running along the 0.25-mile MediaCityUK branch while working from Eccles to Piccadilly on 31 August 2013. Running in the opposite direction towards Manchester was Stagecoach Manchester 19498 (MX09 ASV), an Alexander Dennis Trident Enviro 400, followed by an Arriva North West Optare Solo M880SL (CX57 CYV) that dates from December 2007. The MediaCityUK branch opened for business in 2010.

On a damp autumnal evening, T68 1007 was stood in the single-track terminus at Eccles, awaiting departure with the 21.00 service to Piccadilly via MediaCityUK on 6 November 2013. The Eccles route opened in 1999. No. 1007 was the first tram to traverse the on-street city centre running section in April 1992. It was an appropriate choice as the last Manchester Corporation tram to run through the city streets in 1949 was fleet number 1007. As a consequence, T68 1007 has been reserved for use at the Heaton Park Tramway Museum. No. 1007 was also used on the T68 farewell tour (along with 1016) on 26 May 2014.

T68A 2003 was departing from Altrincham with a service to Bury on 26 July 2013. The two tracks on the left are used exclusively by the Metrolink, while on the other side of the island platform are the two non-electrified lines used by Northern services between Stockport and Chester. There were six T68A trams (2001–2006) introduced in 1999 primarily for use on the Eccles route. The former heavy rail route to Altrincham opened as part of the Metrolink system in 1992.

The former heavy rail Oldham Loop—from Thorpes Bridge Junction, Newton Heath, via Oldham, Shaw, and Crompton to Rochdale—was closed in October 2009 for conversion to the Metrolink. The first section to Shaw opened in June 2012, but as the street running section through Oldham town centre was still under construction, a temporary 'bypass' loop utilising the former BR trackbed through what was once Oldham Mumps station was electrified and a new stop (Oldham Mumps) was built. When the street running section was completed in January 2014, the short length of line via the 'old' Oldham Mumps was abandoned. On a cold 24 March 2013, M5000 3014 was arriving at Oldham Mumps with a Rochdale–St Werburgh's Road service. A small portion of the original station platform still survived.

With the projected expansion of the system and the acquisition of more trams, a new depot with extensive stabling facilities was opened at Old Trafford in 2011. As new Bombardier M5000 trams were delivered, they were commissioned at the depot, and prior to the opening of new lines, the vehicles were kept in secure storage at the depot. On 7 November 2012, 3048 and 3055 were stood with other sister vehicles in the depot yard. The control centre for the system was moved from Queens Road depot to Old Trafford in 2013.

With the line to Manchester Airport curving away to the right, M5000 3091 was passing over the junction on the approach to St Werburgh's Road with an East Didsbury–Rochdale service on 16 October 2018. The line to East Didsbury was opened from St Werburgh's Road in May 2013. This was originally part of the CLC South District Line that ran from Chorlton Junction to Cheadle Heath, which had been closed in 1969.

The end of the line (for now), at East Didsbury on 16 October 2018. M5000 3029 was stood with a service to Rochdale via Exchange Square. The former Cheshire Lines route was reopened from St Werburgh's Road to the island platform terminus at East Didsbury in May 2013. Beyond the end of the line, the original trackbed disappears into the undergrowth, but there have been plans in the past to take the Metrolink onwards towards Stockport. There are 302 car parking spaces available at East Didsbury.

M5000 3067 was approaching the Metrolink terminus at Manchester Airport with a service from Victoria on 16 October 2018. The route to the airport from St Werburgh's Road via Wythenshawe was opened in November 2014. The small terminus is located adjacent to the National Rail platforms at Terminal 2.

With the large Ikea store as a backdrop, M5000s 3092 and 3070 were threading their way out of Ashton-under-Lyne along Lord Sheldon Way (A6140), with a service to Eccles via MediaCityUK on 10 June 2018. The East Manchester route of the Metrolink to Ashton-under-Lyne via Droylsden was opened in October 2013.

M5000 3088 was running alongside the Calder Valley Line as it was approaching the ramp that takes the Metrolink down to street level at Rochdale on 23 August 2016. In the far distance is the ramp to the bridge that takes the Metrolink across the Network Rail tracks to access the former Oldham Loop, which was opened as part of the Metrolink network in March 2014.

Bibliography

Bridge, M., *Track Atlas of Mainland Britain* (Sheffield: Platform 5 Publishing Ltd, 2012)

Gilbert, A. C. and Knight, N. R., *Railways around Manchester* (Manchester: Manchester Transport Museum Society, 1979)

Marshall, J., *Forgotten Railways: North West England* (Newton Abbot: David and Charles Ltd, 1981)

Thomas, S. and Coward A., *The Manchester to Bury 'Lecky' Line and the Class 504 EMU's* (Bacup: Andrew Coward, 2017)

Transport for Greater Manchester website (www.tfgm.com)